ARTISTI CONTEMPORANEI

A cura di Luigi Paolo Finizio

Italo Mussa

MARIE ZOE GREENE - MERCIER

EDIZIONI « SIFRA »

© SIFRA EDITRICE

Copyright 1968

Via Ugo De Carolis, 93 - 00136 Roma

Library of Congress Catalog Card Number: 68-9570

Disegno grafico: Sylvia Franchi

Tavola 1

Orpheus and Eurydice, 1957, bronze, 12 ins.
Coll. Mr. and Mrs. Luis Kutner, Chicago

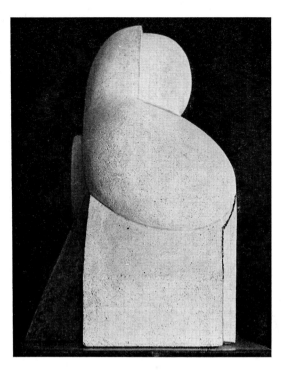

Fig. 1 *Form Encircled, 1945, cement, 18 ins., Coll. Mr. Roy Silverstein, Deerfield, Illinois*

Alle origine della ricerca formale della Greene-Mercier vi è, vivo e operante, un intento artigianale. La struttura che qualifica e forma questa sua operosità artigianale non va intesa solo come bravura che conosce le regole, ma sopratutto come modo di intendere a fruire, nella riflessione, la materia. E nel modo specifico di intuire la materia quale riflessione della mente ed esercizio della mano, la Greene-Mercier ritrova la realtà delle sue opere che sono affatto evocate e plasmate da un compiacimento puramente intellettuale. In esse la realtà non è mediata da innesti polemici, ma è nella « ossatura » e nella « essenzialità » ritmica della forma medesima. Evidentemente la Greene-Mercier, pur avendo vissuto in un paese di prodotti di consumo dove tutt'ora vive, non polemizza con la materia ma stende il classico rapporto a due.

Il materiale prediletto per la realizzaione delle sue sculture è il bronzo. Dunque il modello della sua esperienza è la forma, che è intesa come fonte di energia e come oggetto in cui modellare, nello spazio, una mossa e chiara struttura. Un altro aspetto da considerare è che l'artista ha sempre polemizzato contro l'« informalismo materico ». Alla incertezza o al caso di questa irraggiungibile prospettiva essa ha opposto il dato di fatto.

Ho preferito usare il termine « materiale », anziché « oggetto », per denominare l'opera della Greene-Mercier, perché con essa l'artista manifesta sempre quell'intento costruttivo (artigianale, come dicevo) che conferisce il significato figurativo e gli orizzonti tangibili alla immaginazione. E, che tutto ciò sia vero, è dimostrato dal fatto che le sue opere sono sempre intese come « corpi » esaltanti lo spazio e la luce. Percettivamente le sue forme sono dotate di una riflessa energia in atto, che è chiaramente, come nella serie di opere intitolate « Orfeo e Euridice », (Tav. 1) tutta concentrata nella continuità della linea plastica che si snoda, con un ritmo arabescato, liberamente nello spazio tracciando le immagini nella atmosfera. Il tema principale di essa è appunto di determinare il confine alla nascente

Fig. 2 *Torso in rotation, 1946, bronze, 10 ins., Coll. Dr. and Mrs. Alan D. Green, Wilmette, Illinois*

Fig. 3 *Collage 4, 1946, paer on glass, 15x15 ins., Coll. Mrs. Louis J. A. Mercier, Washington, D.C.*

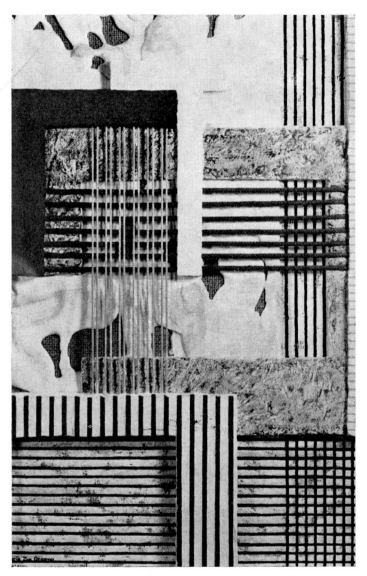

Fig. 4 *Relief 2, 1950, string, plaster and gouache on burlap, 22x15 ins., Coll. of the Artist*

Fig. 5 *Collage* 10, 1947, *paper, string and thread on glass,*
18x20 *ins. Coll. of the Artist*

immagine. L'oggetto, invece aggredisce e mortifica la luce e lo spazio. Quindi se di forme si vuol parlare, esse devono essere intese come una specie di « fogli » trasparenti ritagliati nell'intensità atmosferica e spaziale.

Ma — come in seguito vedremo — la esaltazione dello spazio avrà soluzioni diverse. La linea plastica continua viene sostituita da forme geometriche, le quali tuttavia non obbligano nè condizionano la composizione verso una concezione chiusa dello spazio. Il tema principale rimane sempre la luce e lo spazio, questa volta intesi come contorno e commento della forma: essi non agiscono dall'interno, ma dall'esterno. Ed è proprio questa pressione che determina una giusta struttura ritmica alla intera composizione della scultura.

Per comprendere pienamente il formarsi e svilupparsi del linguaggio nelle sculture della Greene-Mercier (l'artista è anche pittrice) bisogna risalire al 1937, anno in cui frequenta un corso al New Bauhaus di Chicago dove insegnava Moholy-Nagy,

Archipenko, Gyorgy Kepes. L'influenza di questi artisti esercitata sulla scultrice, non è individuabile tanto nelle opere di quel periodo (Archipenko a parte) quanto nel nuovo modo — che darà i suoi frutti alcuni anni più tardi — di elaborare il mezzo materico, di impostare una problematica spaziale, di controllare gli sviluppi intenzionali.

Intensi di attività sia nel campo della ricerca plastica e sia nel campo dell'espressione pittorica sono gli anni 1945-48. Nella forma plastica, che per il modo di unire e innestare le singole parti componenti l'intero corpo scultoreo ricorda quella « archetipa » di Archipenko, le opere « Forme encircled ». (Fig. 1) « Mere et Deux Fils » (Tav. 6) del '45 e « Torso in rotazione » del '46 (Fig. 2) hanno come risultato caratteristico non solo le superfici sporgenti, ma il racchiudersi di un significato remoto che si perde nel tempo. La luce che si accentua e che si rinfrange su di esse, mette in evidenza il loro movimento represso fin dal suo primo insorgere. Più che rappresentare ritmi oggettivi in movimento o imma-

Fig. 6 *Collage* 17, 1953, *paper and rope on glass,* 24x20 *ins., Coll. of the Artist*

gini totemiche, queste sculture ricordano elementi di forme primarie. L'ispirazione è stata la base ideale in cui queste forme hanno attinto il loro significato emblematico. Solo in « Mother and Child » (Tav. 5) del '48, la preferenza di ampi e ondulati piani aperti alla luce, la muta presenza racchiusa nelle sembianze umane denotano una origine iconografica votiva messicana.

Il valore di una espressione spontanea racchiusa nella linea che velocemente delinea la immagine, è nei disegni preparatori di alcune sculture del '52, i quali stilisticamente sviluppano un tema formale in un senso propriamente plastico-lineare. La loro presenza è il sunto di « una preesistente realtà sensibile ». La Greene-Mercier, in questi disegni, ha volupo approfondire emotivamente un tema obbedendo a certe norme riscontrabili nell'ambito storico, ponendo così la propria immaginazione come misura dell'evento lineare.

Non bisogna dimenticare, a questo proposito, che la Greene-Mercier ha compiuto viaggi nel Mes-

sico fin dal 1935, studiandovi l'architettura e la scultura barocca. Quindi certe sue inclinazioni di carattere evocativo formale, si possono considerare alla luce di questi eventi. L'adesione verso una forma chiusa, depositaria di significati umani e religiosi, trova dunque una giustificazione nel campo iconografico.

Il formarsi stilistico delle sue sculture — sopra esaminate — bisogna aggiungere trovò subito due conferme sul piano della esperienza: la prima era nel linguaggio plastico di Archipenko e la seconda nell'immaginazione, che aveva depositato nella sua memoria il ricordo di uno stile antico.

All'esperienza pittorica appartengono, durante gli stessi anni, la serie di opere « Collage » e « Relief ». Qui la ricerca è nettamente diversa, da quella manifestata nella scultura, in quanto gli elementi compositivi sono dei frammenti ritrovati.

La ricomposizione di questi elementi non è affidata tuttavia al caso ma è sempre intenzionalizzata, sia pure in un clima esistenziale che ripercorre il

Tavola 2

*Collage 14, 1952, paper and string on glass,
18x24 ins. Coll. International Film Bureau,
Chicago*

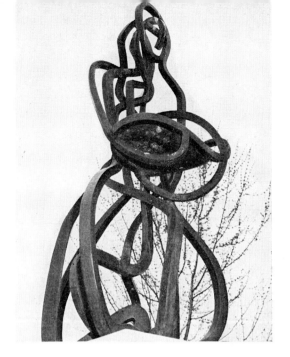

Fig. 7 *The Multiplication of the Loaves and Fishes*, 1946, *bronze, 6 ft., First Baptist Church, Bloomington, Indiana*

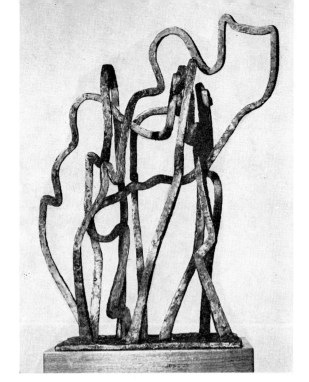

Fig. 8 *Orpheus and Eurydice IV*, 1960, *bronze, 14 ins., Coll. Mrs. Arthur Mostow, Sokie, Illinois*

Fig. 9 *Evolutionary Effort*, 1961, *bronze, 15 ins., Coll. Mrs. Catesby T. Jones, Mayaguez. P. R.*

Fig. 10 *Protection*, 1962, *bronze, 30 ins., Coll. of the Artist*

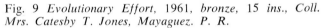

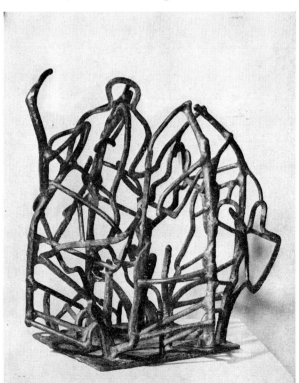

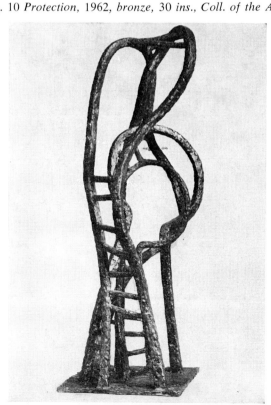

Fig. 11 *Orphée et Eurydice VIII*, 1962, *bronze*, 15 *ins.,
Coll. of the Artist*

ritmo dell'intera composizione. Il loro significato espressivo sembra essere tratto dalla memoria. Infatti, considerando certi ricordi stilistici, è da questi, io credo, che la Greene-Mercier immagina l'invenzione per animare le sue opere. Ogni singolo elemento, nei Collage, trova una sua adeguazione ed espressione significativa nel contesto compositivo. Mentre nei « Relief » (Tav. 3) la materia pittorica anche se è elaborata pittoricamente, è pur sempre legata ad una concezione di natura informale. La superficie pittorica è una superficie esistenzialmente anonima.

A parte il periodo (in scultura) che per i suoi postulati contenutistici abbiamo definito di carattere intellettuale-evocativo, la riflessione della Greene-Mercier si rivolge presto a concezioni più razionali e intenzionali. Quella che era una operosità, come si è detto, di carattere intellettuale-evocativo, si concentra in una intenzionalità creativa. Il processo interiore diviene lo stesso processo del fare, anche se

nel primo permane sempre un *esprit de finesse*. In questi propositi intenzionali anche la scelta dei temi figurativi influisce direttamente su ciò che la scultrice vuol rappresentare: il fine, d'ora in poi, che la Greene-Mercier vuol raggiungere è il formarsi di una immagine da percepirsi liberamente nello spazio, senza la influenza di imposizioni canoniche. E quel fine non può che essere una visione percettiva delle cose. Il fatto stesso di stendere una linea plastica nello spazio, significa che si vuol esprimere qualcosa; la sua importanza sta nella chiarezza e nella essenzialità che ne deduce la percezione.

Su queste premesse la Greene-Mercier sviluppa — attraverso gli anni — la serie di sculture « Orfeo e Euridice », affidando alla sola linea plastica il valore della loro espressione in termini spaziali. La mitica leggenda, che in poesia affida il suo valore semantico alla parola sapiente del poeta, qui diventa oggetto poetico della percezione e a essa si offre come intenzionalità sematica.

Tavola 3

Relief, 1951, plaster on burlap, 16x10 ins. Coll.
Mr. and Mrs. James Rousmaniere, Cambridge,
Mass.

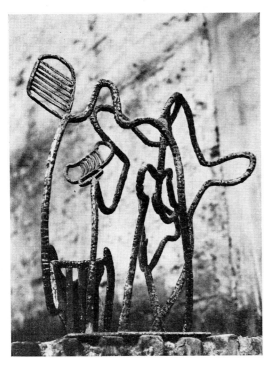

Fig. 12 *Strings and Winds II*, 1964, *bronze, 30 ins., Coll. of the Artist*

Un primo esempio, che tanto ha contribuito a formare lo stile di questa serie di opere, è nell'opera «The multiplication of the loaves and Fiches» (Tav. 9) del '56. In essa le linee in bronzo svolgono una traiettoria in senso verticale come a forare lo spazio e si incurvano energicamente, continuamente all'interno della forma aperta piramidale. Più che rendere la percezione esatta del loro percorso, le linee determinano, e in modo particolare nella parte alta, un groviglio serrato e soffocante che potremmo definire di natura Informale. Il loro andamento, nello spazio, ricorda quello del segno nella pittura informale di gesto di origine espressionista.

L'anno dopo la Greene-Mercier dà inizio alla prima opera di « Orfeo e Euridice » (Tav. 1). Il carattere espressionistico che la linea energetica assume nell'improntare il contorno delle immagini serve sopratutto a sottolineare il movimento dell'intera composizione. I vuoti che si formano nelle immagini sono anch'essi densi di espressione: sembrano chiare ombre fantastiche che giocano con ritmo in-

cessante al chiarore di una luce improvvisa.

Evidentemente l'artista, che piega il bronzo con una capacità artigianale veramente eccezionale, sa che la continuità del suo racconto non può essere affidata alla sola spazialità della linea plastica. Bisogna anche sfruttare lo spazio entro il confine della immagine, altrimenti si corre il rischio di perdersi in un *ludus* itinerante. Ma la sua adattabilità non deve dare luogo ad uno scatenarsi di linee arbitrarie nel movimento e pieni di grovigli negli accordi.

Con questa chiarezza l'artista ha realizzato e considerato le linee plastiche che compongono « Orfeo e Euridice IV » (Tav. 7) del '58. Il loro compenetrarsi continuo nelle immagini non genera l'informe, ma esalta l'intera concezione spaziale del gruppo scultoreo. Il maggior fattore che la percezione deduce è il concentrarsi delle forze, che si piega al ritmo ondulato della linea. E' per da notare che tale concentrazione di forze ritmiche nello spazio è la raratteristica fondamentale di tutta la serie dedicata ad « Orfeo e Euridice ». E questo pieno cre-

Fig. 13 *Strings and Winds I, 1964, bronze, Coll. of the Artist*

scendo si ha nell'« Orfeo e Euridice VIII » del '62 (Fig. 11).

La esaltazione del movimento e il modellare in *plein-air* la ossatura della immagine, sempre concepita come contorno, sono motivi stilistici interpretati metaforicamente: evitando l'oggettualità a priori nel concepire la immagine, essi si danno alla percezione come oggetti da essere interpretati.

Questa ricerca interpretativa, nelle opere « La protection » e « L'element de protection » del '62 è data in partenza. La libera tensione del movimento della linea plastica nello spazio, è soggetta a una costrizione serrata e si staticizza come avviene nelle serpentine ghiacciate. Lo spazio e la luce non esaltano la composizione: gettano i loro opachi riflessi sulle dolenti ossature, come una giornata grigia di autunno sugli alberi spogli. La nostra percezione di fronte a queste opere si spiega su se stessa o si perde nella trappola dei significati che continuamente affiorano dal subconscio.

E', questo, un momento particolare dell'attivi-

tà che riuscendo a giungere direttamente sull'oggetto riflettuto, si è perso in un orbita metafisica.

Prima di esaminare le opere degli anni 1960-67, quelle che per la linea di ricerca si riallacciano alle precedenti, è doveroso ricordare un altro momento particolare dell'attività dell'artista. Esso è caratterizzato da sculture in cui la materia, prima di essere impiegata come elemento costruttivo, viene ridotta in oggetto, più o meno elaborato, che poi viene montato considerando come termine ultimo una sua rappresentazione fantastica. « Container Composition » (Tav. 11) del '65 e la serie intitolata « Perugina » del '66, (Fig. 19,20) per fare solo qualche esempio. Queste opere. sul piano del linguaggio, sono un esempio isolato in quanto la ricerca viene minimizzata e rafforzato il fine rappresentativo.

La linea intenzionale ed artigianale, che è alla base della ricerca della scultrice, risiede nell'opera « The fifthi day », (Fig. 30) bozzetto che è servito a realizzare « Composition for architectural plaza » (Tav. 12) del '67. Qui l'intento artigianale, che è

Tavola 4

*Collage 21, 1954, 24x20 ins. Coll. Mr. and Mrs.
Sydney Stein Jr., Chicago*

Tavola 5

Mother and Child, 1948, bronze, 14 ins. Coll.
Mr. and Mrs. H. Gregg Lewis, Chicago; Rev.
and Mrs. Frank G. Nelson, Chicago

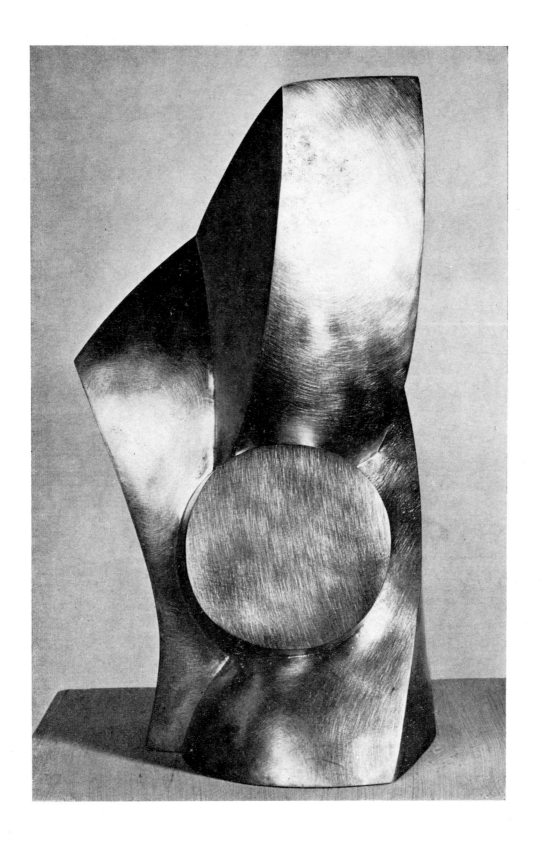

Tavola 6

Mère et deux fils, 1945, bronze. Coll. Mr. Gene Segal, Chicago

Fig. 14 *Strings and Winds III*, 1964, *bronze*, 30 *ins., Coll. of the Artist*

Fig. 15 *Strings and Winds IV*, 1964, *bronze*, 30 *ins., Coll. of the Artist*

anche il carattere della Greene-Mercier è evidente non solo nelle saldature che uniscono i cinque cubi, ma soprattutto nella loro equidistanza da intendersi quale fattore ritmico percettivo. Quello che era il problema del movimento e della continuità dello spazio della linea, diviene ora un problema di rapporti di volumi nello spazio. Essenzializzando in partenza le forme geometriche, che debbono reggersi nello spazio, la Greene-Mercier concepisce il formarsi delle sue composizioni secondo il concetto della sintesi. Esse, infatti, si prestano alla percezione sempre come forme da essere analizzate ed interpretate.

Dunque l'essere nello spazio delle nuove sculture si presenta di una spazialità più oggettiva, impostato com'è sulla ricerca dei rapporti tra i pieni e i vuoti.

A questo punto la ricerca nelle opere della Greene-Mercier compie una svolta: non tanto in senso sostanziale, quanto in modo rappresentativo. Il problema rimane sempre quello visuale ed artigiana-

le. I ritagli di materia, come nell'opera « Marching Figures » del 1967 sono disposti, nello spazio, considerando i loro rapporti volumetrici nel ritmo dei pieni e dei vuoti. Qui anche le ombre assumono uno aspetto di motivo plastico. In questa libertà costruttiva, svincolata da ogni timore figurativo, la Greene-Mercier ritrova il significato della sua esperienza.

Italo Mussa

Fig. 16 *Container composition II, 1965, bronze 16 ins., Coll. of the Artist*

At the source of Marie Zoe Greene-Mercier's experiments with form there in always the lively and operative purpose of suiting means to design, design to material, and material to idea with impeccable execution. The factors which inform and qualify this artisan aspect of her activity must not be understood as simply a bravura which knows all the rules, but rather more as a way of understanding her materials and using them perceptively. And it is precisely in this feeling for materials, in this union of the intuitive intelligence and the trained hand, that Greene-Mercier finds the true bent of her works, which are evoked and shaped, in fact, with that pleasure which is purely of the intellect. The reality of these works does not come indirectly from superimposed polemics, but from the « bone-structure » and the rhythmical « essentiality » of the form itself. Obviously Greene-Mercier, although she has lived all her life in a country of mass-produced consumer products, and still lives there, does not struggle with her materials, but carries the classic rapport a little further. Her preferred material for the realization of her sculptures is bronze. Thus form has been the chief concern in her experience: form understood as a source of energy, and as an object with which to set up a clear and moving structure in space. Another aspect of this artist which we must consider is that she has always taken exception to « informality » as applied to the employment of material. To the uncertainty and reliance on chance of the free or improvised approach, she has always opposed the aim of precision, knowledge, and flawless execution.

I have preferred to use the terms « material » and « object » in speaking of Greene-Mercier's work, since in this artist there is always manifest the structural intent which confers the figurative significance and the tangible outlines on her imaginative idea. The truth of this is demonstrated by the fact that her forms are always conceived as «bodies» exalting light and space. Her forms are perceptively endowed with a reflection of live energy, which is

Fig. 17 *Orpheus and Eurydice* XV, 1965, *bronze, 4 ft. Coll. of the Artist*

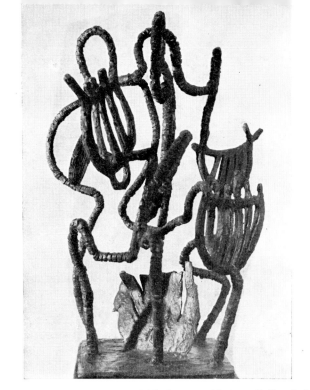

Fig. 18 *The Musicians*, 1965, *bronze, 22 ins. Coll. of the Artist*

Fig. 19 *Perugina III*, 1966, *bronze, 40 ins., Coll. of the Artist*

Fig. 20 *Perugina I*, 1966, *bronze, 30 ins. Coll. of the Artist*

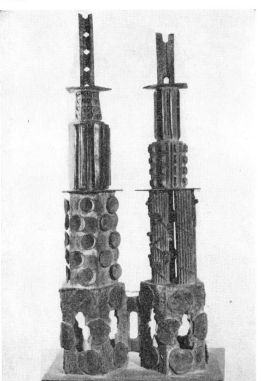

Fig. 21 *The Musicians II,* 1966, *bronze, 23 ins. Coll. of the Artist*

clearly, as in the series of works called *Orpheus and Eurydice,* (Pl. 1) completely concentrated in the continuity of the plastic line which unwinds freely in space with an arabesque rhythm, tracing the shapes in the air. The principle theme lies precisely in determining the outlines of the emerging image. An object, however, assaults and belittles light and space. Thus if we are going to speak of forms here we must consider them as some sort of transparent « sheets » or « pages » cut out in the intensity of space and atmosphere.

But — as we shall see later — the exaltation of space will have various solutions in Greene-Mercier's work. The continuous plastic line sometimes gives over to geometric form, but this never obliges or drives the composition toward a closed concept of space. The chief subject remains ever light and space, but this time seen as surrounding and commenting on the form: not acting from within, but from without. And it is this very pressure from without which determines the just rhythmical balance of the entire composition of the sculpture.

To fully understand the formation and devlopment of Greene-Mercier's sculptural language, we must note that in 1937 she frequented the New Bauhaus in Chicago when Moholy-Nagy, Archipenko and Gyorgy Kepes were teaching there. The influence of these artists upon the sculptress is not so evident in her work of that period (Archipenko apart) so much as it is in her new way — to bear fruit some years later — of working with her materials, of setting up spatial problems, of controlling her planned development of the work at hand.

The years 1945-48 were intensely active, both in the creation of free-standing sculptures and in the invention of three-dimensional polychromed relief and collages of many and mixed materials. The free-standing sculpture, in its way of uniting and superimposing the simple component parts of the composition, recalls the basic elements of Archipenko's style: the works *Form Encircled,* (fig. 1) *Mother and Two Sons,* (Pl. 6) both of 1945, and the *Torso*

29

Fig. 22 *Orpheus and Eurydice* XVI, *1966, bronze, 50 ins.,*
Coll. of the Artist

in Rotation of 1946 (fig. 2) have the noticeable characteristics not only of projecting surfaces, but seem to contain within themselves a remote meaning which is lost in time. The light which is accentuated in these works, and reflected from them, reveals that their movement has been considered and controlled from the first. Rather than representing the rhythm of objects in motion or totemic images, these sculptures evoke elements of primary forms. Imaginative inspiration has been the basis from which these forms have derived their emblematic significance. Only in *Mother and Child,* (Pl. 5) 1948, with its preference for ample and undulating planes open to the light, and the mute presence locked in the semblance of human form, do we find what suggests a specific origin: iconographic, votive, Mexican.

The value of spontaneous expression captured in the line which rapidly shapes the image is already seen in preliminary drawings, for some sculptures of 1952, which develop a formal theme stylistically in a truly plastic-linear sense. Their presence is the summing-up of a « pre-existent tangible reality ». Greene-Mercier, in these drawings, sought to probe a theme emotionally while obeying ascertainable historical norms, posing her own imagination as the measure of the linear occurence.

In regard to this we must not forget that Greene-Mercier had already traveled in Mexico in 1935, studying architecture and Baroque sculpture. Thus certain of her inclinations of a formal evocative nature can be considered in the light of those facts. Her adherence to a closed form, repository of human and religious significances, finds a justification in the iconographic field.

The stylistic formation of her sculpture, which we have examined above, found at once two confirmations on the plane of past experience: the first was in the plastic language of Archipenko and the second in her own imagination, which had lodged in her memory the recollection of an antique style.

To a more pictorial experience belong the

30

Fig. 23 *The Burning Bush I, 1966, bronze, 10 ins., Coll. of the Artist*

Fig. 24 *Burning Bush V, 1966, bronze, 26 ins. Coll. of the Artist*

series of collages and reliefs (three-dimensional raised-surface mixed-medium works) executed during the same years. Here the artist sought something quite different from the experiments manifest in her sculpture, since here the compositional elements are mostly *objets trouvés,* fragments picked up here and there.

The recomposition of these « found » elements is not, however, entrusted to chance but is always intentional, although an existential climate permeates the rhythm of the entire composition. Their expressive significance seems to be dealt from memory. In fact, considering certain stylistic souvenirs, it is from them, I think, that Greene-Mercier gives shape to the invention which animates her work. Every single element, in the collages, (fig. 3, 5, 6) finds its proportion and its expressive significance in the compositional context. While in the reliefs (Pl. 3) the pictorial matter, even if it is elaborated pictorially, is nevertheless always bound to a conception of a non-formal nature. The pictorial surface is an essentially anonymous surface.

Apart from the period in sculpture which, by its postulates concerning content, we have defined as being of an intellectual-evocative character, Greene-Mercier's thought turned quickly toward more rational and more intentional compositional concepts. That manner of working which was intellectual-evocative fused itself into a creative intention. The interior process became the same process as the doing, even if in the first persists an *esprit de finesse.* With these thought-out purposes the choice of figurative themes directly influences that which the sculptress wishes to represent; from now on Greene-Mercier's goal is the formation of an image freely perceived in space without the influence of imposed canons. And that goal can only be a perceptive vision of things. The mere fact of extending a plastic line in space signifies that the artist wishes to express something. Its importance lies in the clarity and economy which the spectator perceives in it.

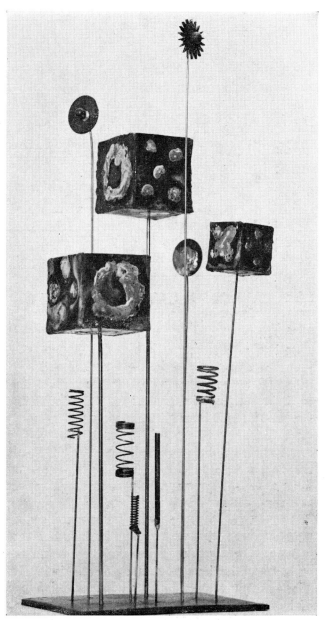

Fig. 25 *Garden Figures, 1968, welded steel and brass, 20 ins. Coll. Mr. and. Mrs. Dallas G. Alinder, New York*

Fig. 26 *Tree and Fruit, 1965, brass, welded and brazed steel, Coll. Miss. Elizabeth Jane Foster, Naples*

Tavola 7

Orpheus and Eurydice V, 1958, bronze, 14 ins.
Coll. Mr. and Mrs. Robert B. Uretz, Chicago

Fig. 27 *Burning Bush II, 1966, bronze, 13 ins., Coll. of the Artist*

Fig. 28 *Burning Bush VII, 1966, bronze, 13 ins., Coll of the Artist*

On these premises Greene-Mercier has developed over the years her series of sculptures, *Orpheus and Eurydice,* where she entrusts to the plastic line alone the weight of its expression in spatial terms. The myth, which in poetry has its semantical value in the wise words of the poet, here becomes the poetical object of perception and offers itself with semantical purpose.

A first example, which contributed so much to forming the style of this series, is in the work *The Multiplication of the Loaves and Fishes* (Pl. 9) of 1956. In this the lines of the bronze shoot up vertically as if to pierce and puncture space, then curve forcefully inward upon themselves, continually developing within the open pyramidal form. Rather than rendering the exact perception of their passage, the lines define, especially in the upper part of the sculpture, a dense, suffocating tangle which we might describe as Non-formal in nature. Their progress in space recalls certain elements in non-formal action painting of abstract-expressionist origins.

The year following Greene-Mercier initiated the first work (Pl. 1) of the *Orpheus and Eurydice* cycle. The expressionistic character which the forceful line assumes in delineating the outlines of the images serves most of all to underline the movement of the entire composition. The empty spaces which are thus formed in the images are equally dense with expression: they seem pale fantastic shadows which play with an unceasing rhythm in the clarity of an improvised light.

It is obvious that the artist, who bends the bronze to her purpose with a truly exceptional virtuosity, knows that the continuity of her tale cannot be entrusted to the spatial quality of the plastic line alone. It is necessary also to exploit the space within the contines of the image, otherwise one runs the risk of losing oneself in an errant playfulness. Yet her adaptability is such that she never allows the unleashing of arbitary lines or entanglements in the arrangements.

With this clarity the artist has considered and

Fig. 29 *Marching Figure II*, 1967, *bronze*, 10 *ins. Coll. Dr. and Mrs. R. Gerald Suskind, Washington, D.C.*

realized the plastic lines which make up the *Orpheus and Eurydice* (Pl. 7) of 1958. Their continuous interpenetration in the images does not generate a non-formal effect, but emphasizes the entire spatial conception of the sculptural group. The major factor which the spectator grasps is the concentration of forces which bend to the wavy rhythm of the line. And indeed we must note that such a concentration of rhythmical forces in space is the fundamental charateristic of the whole series dedicated to *Orpheus and Eurydice*. And this, in full crescendo, we see in the *Orpheus and Eurydice* VIII of 1962 (fig. 11).

The exaltation of movement and the modelling in the open air of the basic structure of the image, always conceived as an outline, are stylistic motives interpreted metaphorically: avoiding *a priori* objectuality in conceiving the image, these figures offer themselves to the perceptive viewer as objects to be interpreted.

This need to interpret, in the work *Protection*

(fig. 10) of 1962, is obvious from the outset. The free tension of the plastic line moving in space is subjected to a close constriction because of the series of horizontal rungs confining the design which becomes as static as the windings of a frozen stream. Space and light here do not point up the composition: they cast their opaque shadows on the afflicted structure, like a grey day in autumn lights the leafless trees. Our perception of this work turns in on itself or is lost in the trap of meanings which continuously rise from the subconscious. This is a particular moment in the activity of the artist in which her intent and purpose do not succeed in directly reaching the object, but loses itself in a metaphysical orbit.

Before examining the works of the years 1960-67, those which in their line of experiment and enquiry are related to the preceding, we must consider another particular moment in the activity of this artist. It is characterized by sculpture in which the material, before being utilized as a constructive

36

Tavola 8

Orpheus and Eurydice XIV, 1965, bronze, 5ft.
Coll. of the Artist

Fig. 30 *The fifth day*, 1967, *brazed steel, 15 ins., Coll. Mr. Robert Korach, Chicago*

element, is reduced to objects, more or less elaborated, to be assembled with the ultimate goal of a fanciful representation of their own. *Container Composition* (Pl. 11) in 1965 and the series called *Perugina* (fig. 19, 20) in 1966, to give only these examples. These works, on the language plane, are isolated examples in which experiment and enquiry are minimized and the representational end reinforced.

The purposeful, intentional line, the authority of knowledgable execution which is at the base of this artist's quest, continues in the work *The Fifth Day,* (fig. 30) a sketch in welded steel which served to realize *Composition for Architectural Plaza.* (Pl. 12) Here the preoccupation with quality of execution which is characteristic of Greene-Mercier is evident not only in the welded square tubing which unites the five cubes, but also in the calculated equidistance of the cubes from one another, intended as a factor in the perceptual rhythms. That which was a problem of movement and of the continuity of line in space,

now becomes a problem of the relationship of volume in space. Simplifying from the first the geometrical forms that will rise in space, Greene-Mercier undertakes the formation of her compositions according to the concept of synthesis. They always present themselves to the perception as forms to be analyzed and interpreted.

Thus the existence in space of her new sculptures shows a more objective study of space relationships, imposed as it is on her enquiries into the relations between volume and empty space.

At this point the investigations revealed in Greene-Mercier's work complete a turn: not so much in their essentials as in the representational manner. The problems remain still those of the visual elements and the disposing of them in orderly configurations. The lengths of material, as in the work *Marching Figures* of 1957, (fig. 29) are disposed in space with a fine sense of their volumetric relationships in the play of volume and empty space. Here the shadows, too, assume a plastic mo-

Fig. 31 *Burning Bush*, 1967, *welded brass and steel*, 14 *ins.*
Coll. Mr. and Mrs. George B. Gillespie, Springfield, Illinois

Fig. 32 *In a Pear Tree*, 1967, *brazed steel and brass*, 16 *ins., Coll. Mr. Michael Sorkin, Chicago*

tive. In this constructive liberty, which has shaken off every figurative timidity, Greene-Mercier finds the meaning of her total personal experience.

Italo Mussa

(Translated by Eugene Walter)

Tavola 9

The Multiplication of the Loaves and Fishes,
1956, bronze, 6ft. Coll. First Baptist Church,
Bloomington, Indiana

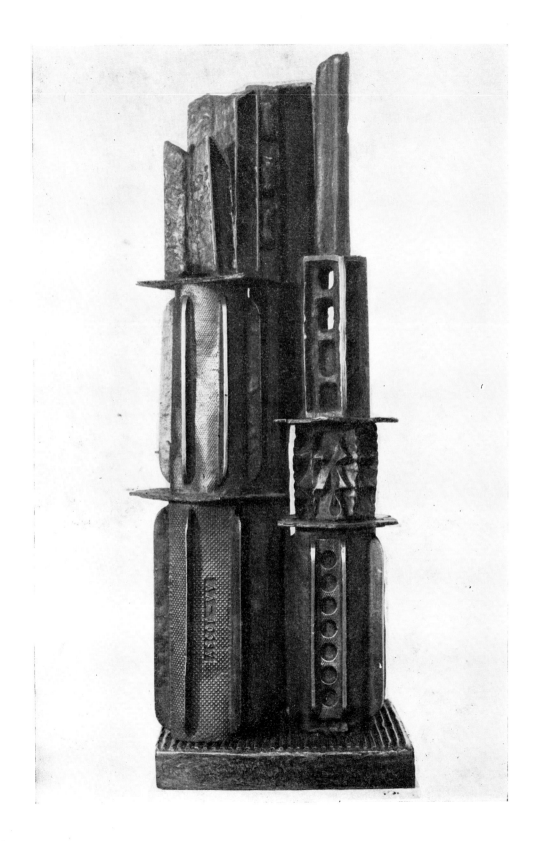

Tavola 10

Perugina II, 1966, bronze, 25 ins. Coll. of the Artist

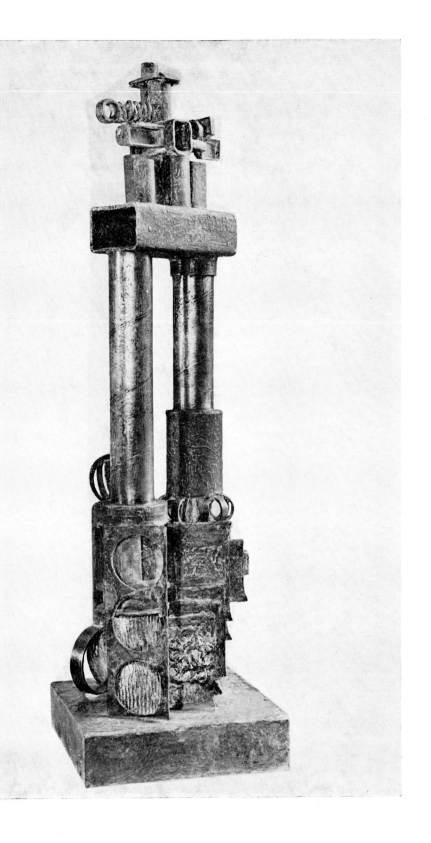

Tavola 11

Container Composition, 1965, bronze, 50 ins.
Coll. Mr. and Mrs. Marvin N. Stone, Chicago

Tavola 12

Composition for Architectural Plaza, 1967, masonite, II ft.

CURRICULUM VITAE

1911. Nata in U.S.A. da genitori francesi.

1911-33. Vive a Cambridge, Massachusetts, dove il padre, Louis J. A. Mercier, professore di francese, insegnava all'Università di Harvard e a Radcliffe College.

1928-29. Studia in Roma alla Villa Santa Teresa delle Sorelle francese della Santa Unione dei Sacri Cuori.

1929. Viaggia in Italia, Svizzera, Francia, Inghilterra.

1930-33. Si laurea in arte al Radcliffe College, Harvard University. (1931-32 Borsa di studio James and Augusta Barnard, 1932 primo premio nel concorso « Storia di Natale »).

1933-34. Le sono affidate dall'Art Institute di Chicago delle ricerche su artisti francesi dell'ottocento per il « Catalogue of a Century of Progress Exhibition of Paintings and Sculpture ». The Art Institute of Chicago, 1934).

1935. Viaggia per tre mesi nel Messico studiando l'architettura e la scultura barocca coloniale Messicana. Ne presenta uno studio al Dipartimento di Belle Arti al New York University il quale le vince una borsa di studio.

1936. Studia tre mesi in Parigi.

1937-38. Studia al New Bauhaus di Chicago con borsa di studio con L. Moholy-Nagy, Alessandro Archipenko, Gyorgy Kepes.

1939-40. E' impiegata dall'Art Institute di Chicago per conferenze sulla grande mostra d'arte Italiana del Rinascimento inviato dal Governo Italiano. E' autrice di due guide per ragazzi, una sulla mostra Italiana e l'altra su certe opere nella collezione permanente.

1939-41. Vari corsi di scultura al School of the Art Institute of Chicago, California School of Fine Arts San Francisco, Norton Gallery and School of Art, West Palm Beach, Florida.

1941-46. Abita ed espone nel Canadà, a Montreale ed Ottawa.

1945. Vince il secondo posto al National Arts Club, New York, nella mostra per giovani di trentacinque anni o meno. Dal 1946 abita ed espone in Chicago.

1959-62. E' presidente dell'Artists Equity Association di Chicago.

1962-64. E' primo vice-presidente dell'Associazione Nazionale, Artists Equity Association, Seattle, Washington.

1966. Abita in Italia.

1968. Vince un primo premio di scultura, categoria composizione e una Medaglia d'argento al III Salon International de la Femme, Cannes, Francia. Dal 1961 ogni anno abita e lavora qualche mese in Italia con viaggi frequenti in Francia, Austria, Svizzera, Germania, Belgio, Inghilterra.

BIOGRAPHICAL NOTES

1911. Born in the United States of French parents.

1911-33. Grew up in Cambridge, Massachusetts, where her father, Louis J. A. Mercier, was associate Professor of French and Education at Harvard University and Radcliffe College.

1928-29. Studied in Rome at the French School, Villa Santa Teresa.

1929. Travelled in Italy, Switzerland, France and England.

1930-33. Obtained an A.B. in Fine Arts at Radcliffe College. (In 1931-32 was awarded a James and Augusta Barnard scholarship and in 1932 worn first prize in the annual Christmas story competition).

1933-34. Researched entries for eighteenth century French paintings for the « Catalogue of a Century of Progress Exhibition of Paintings and Sculpture » The Art Institute of Chicago, 1934.

1935. Spent three months of study in Mexico on colonial Baroque sculpture and architecture and outlined a thesis project which won her a Department scholarship in Fine Arts at New York University.

1936. Studied three months in Paris.

1937-38. With a scholarship grant, studied at the New Bauhaus, Chicago, with L. Moholy-Nagy, Alexander Archipenko, Gyorgy Kepes.

1939-40. Was lecturer for the Department of Education at the Art Institute of Chicago at the Exhibition of Italian Masterpieces loaned by the Italian Government. Wrote a young peoples' workbook and guide to the exhibition followed by a second book for the Department on selected work of the permanent collection of the museum.

1939-41. Followed sculpture courses with Albin Polasek at the Art Institute of Chicago, Frank Stackpole at the California School of Fine Arts, and at the Norton School of Art, West Palm Beach, Florida.

1941-46. Worked and exhibited in Canada.

1945. Won second place at the National Arts Club, New York, in the annual Exhibition for young artists 35 years or under. Since 1946 has lived in Chicago where she has exhibited regularly.

1959-62. Served as president of the Chicago Chapter of Artists Equity Association.

1962-64. Served as first vice-president of the national organization.

1966. Spent a full year of work and exhibition in Italy.

1968. Won a first prize in sculpture and Silver Medal at the 3rd International Salon of Women Artists in Cannes, France. Since 1961 has spent a good part of every year working and exhibiting in Italy and France.

MOSTRE PERSONALI

1946. Photographic Stores, Ltd. Ottawa, Canada.

1949. Well of the Sea Gallery, Chicago.

1950. Southwest Missouri State College, Springfield, Missouri. Argent Gallery, New York City. American National Theatre Playhouse, New York City. (Single exhibit of Head of Dame Judith Anderson as Clytemnestra in Robinson Jeffers' « Tower Beyond Tragedy » during the run of the play).

1951. Marguerite Hobenberg Gallery, Chicago. Layton Gallery and School of Art, Milwaukee, Wisconsin. Westwinds Bookshop and Gallery, Duxbury, Massachusetts. Newton Center Women's Club, Newton Center, Massachusetts.

1952. Marguerite Hobenberg Gallery, Chicago.

1955. The Art Institute of Chicago, Department of Prints and Drawings.

1956. The Chicago Public Library, Art Department.

1957. American Institute of Architects, Chicago Chapter Office.

1958. Graphic Workshop and Print Gallery, Chicago.

1963. Galerie Raymond Duncan, Paris,

1965. Galleria d'Arte Arno, Firenze.

Fig. 34 *Container Composition VIII*, 1968, *bronze*, 6 *ft.,*
Coll. of the Artist

Fig. 33 *Festal Tree*, 1967, *brazed steel and brass*, 16 *ins.,*
Coll. Dr. Edward Futterman, Chicago

1966. Galleria Numero, Milano,
   Galleria Numero, Roma.
   Galleria Numero, Venezia.
1968. Galleria S. Stefano, Venezia.

MOSTRE COLLETTIVE

1945

National Arts Club, New York.
Royal Canadian Academy, Museum of Fine Arts. Montreal.
Institute of Contemporary Art, Boston, Members' Exhibition.
Audubon Artists Fourth Annual, National Academy Galleries, New York.
Federation of Canadian Artists Gallery, Ottawa.
North Shore Arts Association, East Gloucester, Massachusetts.

1946

National Arts Club, New York.
Federation of Canadian Artists Gallery, Ottawa.
North Shore Arts Association, East Gloucester, Massachusetts.
Cambridge Art Association Annual, Cambridge, Massachusetts.
Evanston Art Center, Chicago Society of Artists, Evanston, Illinois.
Museum of Fine Arts, 63rd Annual Spring Exhibition, Montreal.
Busch Reisinger Museum, Harvard University, Cambridge Centennial Exhibition, Cambridge, Massachusetts.

1947

The Art Institute of Chicago, 58th National American Exhibition.
Renaissance Society at the University of Chicago, Professional Members' Exhibition.
Harvard University, Robinson Hall, Cambridge Art Association.
Evanston Art Center, Chicago Society of Artists, Evanston, Illinois.
Marshall Field Galleries, Chicago Society of Artists, Chicago.
Museum of Fine Arts, 64th Annual Spring Exhibition, Montreal.
North Shore Arts Association, East Gloucester.

1948

The Art Institute of Chicago, 53rd Annual Exhibition of Artists of Chicago and Vicinity.
The Renaissance Society at the University of Chicago, the Exhibition « Sculptors and Sculptors' Drawings ».
Mandel Brothers Gallery, Chicago Society of Artists, Chicago.
Cambridge Art Association, Cambridge, Massachusetts.
North Shore Arts Association East Gloucester, Massachusetts.
Public Library, Dekalb, Illinois, Chicago Society of Artists.

1949

North Shore Arts Association, East Gloucester, Massachusetts.
Harvard University, Robinson Hall, Cambridge Art Association.
Chicago Society of Artists.
The Renaissance Society at the University of Chicago, Professional Members.

1950

Busch Reisinger Museum, Harvard University, Cambridge Art Association.
Boris Mirski Gallery, Boston, Massachusetts.
The Renaissance Society at the University of Chicago, Professional Members.

Third Annual 57th Street Art Fair, Chicago.
Hyde Park Art Center, Professional Artists Exhibit.

1951

Renaissance Society at the University of Chicago, First « Young Collectors » Exhibition.
Boris Mirski Gallery, Boston.
Mandel Brothers Gallery, Chicago.
Mandel Brothers Gallery, Chicago Society of Artists.
Busch Reisinger Museum, Harvard University, Cambridge Art Association.
Renaissance Society at the University of Chicago, Professional Members.
Fourth Annual 57th Street Art Fair, Chicago.
Riverside Museum, New York, Chicago Society of Artists.
Marguerite Hohenberg Gallery, Chicago.

1952

The Art Institute of Chicago, 56th Annual Exhibition of Artists of Chicago and Vicinity.
American Federation of Arts, Travelling Exibition through Midwest Colleges and Universities.
Wellons Gallery, New York City.
Boris Mirski Gallery, Boston.
Marguerite Hohenberg Gallery, Chicago.
Salon des Beaux Arts, Grand Palais des Champs Elysées, Paris.
Salon des Indépendants, Grand Palais des Champs Elysées, Paris.

1953

Renaissance Society at the University of Chicago « Contemporary Sculpture by Chicago Artists ».
1020 Art Center, Chigaco.
University of Chicago, Rockefeller Chapel, « An Exihibition of Religious Art ».
Invitational Exhibition of 18 Chicago Area Artists at the home of Architect Laurence Amstadter, AIA.
Boris Mirski Gallery, Boston.
Wellons Gallery, New York.
Marguerite Hohenberg Gallery, Chicago.
Renaissance Society at the University of Chicago, Professional Members.
Arts Club of Chicago, Professional Members.
Boston Museum of Fine Arts, Society for Independent Artists.

1954

Institute of Design, Momentum Mid-Continental Exhibition, Chicago.
1020 Art Center, Chicago.
Royal Institute Galleries, London, England.
Arts Club of Chicago, 34th Exhibition by Professional Members.
Boris Mirski Gallery, Boston.
Radcliffe College, Exhibition for the 75th Anniversary, Cambridge, Massachusetts.
The Art Institute of Chicago, Art Rental and Sales Collection.
Renaissance Society at the University of Chicago, Professional Members.

1955

The Art Institute of Chicago, Society for Contemporary Art.
The Art Institute of Chicago, Art Rental and Sales Collection.
The Arts Club of Chicago, Professional Members Annual.
The Renaissance Society at the University of Chicago, Professional Members.

1956

Exhibition Momentum, Chicago.
Arts Club of Chicago, Professional Members.
Renaissance Society at the University of Chicago, Professional Members.

1957

Robert North Gallery, Chicago.
Sacred Heart School, Religious Art Exhibition, Hubbard Woods, Illinois.
57th Street Art Fair, Chicago.
Renaissance Society at the University of Chicago, Professional Members.

1958

Myrtle Todes Gallery, Highland Park, Illinois.
Ravinia Festival Art Exhibition, Ravinia, Illinois.
The Renaissance Society at the University of Chicago, Professional Members.
The Arts Club of Chicago, Professional Members.
The Little Gallery, Chicago.

1959

The University of Chicago, May Festival of the Arts, Outdoor Sculpture Exhibition.
Renaissance Society at the University of Chicago, Professional Members.
The Arts Club of Chicago, Professional Members.
The Little Gallery, Chicago.

1960

Kenwood Open House and Garden Exhibition, Chicago.
Renaissance Society at the University of Chicago, Professional Members.
The Arts Club of Chicago, Professional Members.
Michael Zolpe Gallery, Evanston, Illinois.
Baptist Graduate Student Center, First Annual Religious Art Exhibition, Chicago.
Hyde Park Methodist Church, Chicago.
The University of Chicago, Department of Art, Lexington Hall.

1961

Galleria l'88, Roma.
Renaissance Society at the University of Chicago, Exhibition « Faces and Figures ».
Red Door Gallery, Chicago.
Baptist Graduate Student Center, Second Annual Religious Art Exhibition, Chicago.
Illinois State Museum, North Mississippi Valley Artists Exhibition, Springfield, Illinois.
Portrait Center, Chicago.
The Arts Club of Chicago, Professional Members.
The Renaissance Society at the University of Chicago, Professional Members.
Park Forest Art Center, Park Forest, Illinois.
Northwestern University, Methodist Student Foundation, Evanston, Illinois.
University of Illinois, Chicago.
St. James Cathedral, Episcopal, Chicago.
Unitarian Church of Evanston. Evanston, Illinois.
Epworth Methodist Church, Chicago.

The Meadows Club, Chicago.
McKerr Observatory Gallery, Chicago.
The University of Chicago, Woodward Commons.
Michael Zolpe Gallery, Evanston, Illinois.
The Little Gallery, Madison, Wisconsin.
The University of Chicago, Pierce Hall.

1962

Salon d'Automne, Grand Palains des Champs Elysées, Paris.
Galleria l'88, Roma.
Four Arts Gallery, Evanston, Illinois.
The Arts Club of Chicago, Professional Members.
The Renaissance Society at the University of Chicago, Professional Members.
Merchants and Manufacturers Club, Chicago.
The University of Chicago, Woodward Commons.
The Meadows Club, Chicago.
Oak Park and River Forest Township High School, Oak Park, Illinois.
South Shore Gallery, Chicago.
Illinois Institute of Technology, Grover M. Herman Student Union, Chicago.
Evanston Art Center, Evanston, Illinois.
Contemporary Art Workshop, Chicago.

1963

Galerie d'Atri, Paris.
Galerie Alençon, Paris.
L'Union des Artistes et Amateurs d'Art, Paris.
Hotel de Ville, Calais, France.
Arts Club of Chicago, Professional Members.
Northwestern University, Hillel Foundation Gallery, Evanston, Illinois.
State Office Building, Art in Government Exhibit, Springfield, Illinois.
Four Arts Gallery, Evanston, Illinois.
American Baptist Assembly, Religious Art Exhibition, Green Lake, Wisconsin.

1964

South Shore Commission Art League, « Jurors' Show », Chicago.
Galerie d'Atri, Paris.
L'Union des Artistes et Amateurs d'Art, Paris.
Galleria d'Arte Arno, Firenze.
The Arts Club of Chicago, Professional Members,

1965

Gallerie Jacques Casanova, Paris.
Galleria d'Arte Arno, Firenze.
The Arts Club of Chicago, Professional Members.
Musée Rodin, Paris, Salon de la Jeune Sculpture.

1966

Galleria Numero, Firenze, « Operazione Confronti ».
United State Consular Residence, Trieste.
Galleria Schneider, Roma.
Seconda Mostra Internazionale di Scultura all'Aperto, Legnano.
Galeria Jacques Casanova, Paris.
Galleria d'Arte Arno, Firenze.
The Arts Club of Chicago, Professional Members.

Seconda Mostra Internazionale d'Arte Sacra, Trieste.
Renaissance Society at the University of Chicago, « Young Collectors ».
Chicago Society of Artists Gallery, Artists Equity Association, Exhibition for Florentine Flood Relief, Chicago.
Womens' American ORT, Highland Park, Illinois.
Museo all'Aperto, Legnano.

1967

Galerie Jacques Casanova, Paris.
Arts et Beaux Arts, Paris.
Galleria d'Arte Arno, Firenze.
Franz Bader Gallery, Washington, D.C.
VIII Annual Religious Art Exhibition, Baptist Graduate Student Center, Chicago.
Womens' American ORT, Highland Park, Illinois.
Illinois State Museum, XX North Mississippi Valley Exhibition, Springfield, Illinois.
The Arts Club of Chicago, 47th Exhibition by Professional Membres.
Marina City, VII New Horizons in Sculpture Exhibition, Chicago.
Renaissance Society at the University of Chicago, « Young Collectors ».
United States Consular Residence, Trieste.
Museo all'Aperto, Legnano.

1968

Museum of Contemporary Art, Chicago, Exhibition « Made with Paper », Container Corporation of America.
City Museum of Art, St. Louis, Missouri, « Made with Paper ».
Hemisfair 1968, San Antonio, Texas, « Made with Paper ».
Galerie Jacques Casanova, Paris.
Arts et Beaux Arts, Paris.
Galleria d'Arte Arno, Firenze.
Franz Bader Gallery, Washington, D.C.
The Arts Club of Chicago, 48th Exhibition by Professional Members.
United States Consular Residence, Trieste.
III me Salon International del La Femme, Casino Municipale Cannes, France.
Casino Municipale di Cannes.

COLLEZIONI

Southwest Missouri State College, Springfield, Missouri.
Roosevelt University, Chicago, Illinois.
First Baptist Church, Bloomington, Indiana.
First Baptist Church, Chicago.
International Film Bureau, Chicago.
Dr. and Mrs. Leo Alexander, Boston, Massachusetts.
Mrs. Helen T. Bevans, Washington, D.C.
Mr. and Mrs. Lloyd Morain, San Francisco, California.
Mrs. George P. Metcalf, Duxbury, Massachusetts.
Mr. and Mrs. Sydney Stein, Jr., Chicago.
Mr. and Mrs. H. Gregg Lewis, Chicago.
Dr. and Mrs. Joseph Creanza, Chicago.
Mr. and Mrs. Albert Dykema, Chicago.
Mrs. Edward P. Doyle, Chicago.
Mr. and Mrs. Raymond Epstein, Chicago.
Mrs. Marcus A. Hirschl, Chicago.
Mrs. Catesby T. Jones, Mayaguez, Puerto Rico.
Mr. and Mrs. Luis Kutner, Chicago.

Rev. and Mrs. Frank G. Nelson, Chicago.
Mr. and Mrs. Samuel H. Nerlove, Santa Monica, California.
Mr. Charles Oesterreicher, Chicago.
Miss Christine Pertile, Chicago.
Mr. and Mrs. James Rousmaniere, Cambridge, Massachusetts.
Mr. and Mrs. Felix Shuman, Chicago.
Mr. Gene Segal, Chicago.
Mr. Frederick G. Schab, New York.
Mr. and Mrs. Joseph Lederer, Chicago.
Mrs. Louis J. A. Mercier, Chevy Chase, Maryland.
Mr. and Mrs. Steven H. Greene, Sudbury, Massachusetts.
Mr. and Mrs. Theodore H. Lassagne, Glendale, California.
Mr. Robert Korach, Chicago.
Dr. Edward H. Futterman, Chicago.
Mr. and Mrs. George B. Gillespie, Springfield, Illinois.
Miss Carol Korach, Chicago.
Miss Elizabeth Jane Foster, Roma.
Mr. and Mrs. Marvin N. Stone, Stone Container Corporation, Chicago.
Mrs. Arthur Mostow, Skokie, Illinois.
Mrs. and Mrs. Robert B. Uretz, Chicago.
Mr. and Mrs. Henry T. Kakehashi, Chicago.
Mrs. Doris Ambrose, Chicago.
Mr. Edward J. Cory, San Francisco, California.
Dr. and Mrs. Alan D. Green, Wilmette, Illinois.
Miss Jeanne M. Mercier, Chevy Chase, Maryland.
Mrs. John Hirsch, Chicago.
Mr. and Mrs. E. Hector Coates, Chicago.
Mr. and Mrs. J. Bryan Allin, Chicago.
Rev. and Mrs. Ralph W. Reynolds, Chicago.
Mrs. June Lukosh Kahler, Chicago.
Mr. and Mrs. Howard W. Dougherty, Summit, Illinois.
Mrs. Mary E. Druliner, Wilmette, Illinois.
Dr. and Mrs. P. Gerald Suskind, Washington, D.C.
Mr. and Mrs. Lawrence S. P. Hanchek, Glenview, Illinois.
Mr. and Mrs. Bainbridge Crist, Washington, D.C.
Mr. Roy Silverstein, Deerfield, Illinois.
Mr. Michael Sorkin, Chicago.
Mr. and Mrs. Robert Spring, Flushing N.Y.
Mr. and Mrs. Norman H. Liben, Valley Stream, New York.
Mr. James W. Newell, New York.
Mr. and Mrs. Dallas G. Alinder, New York.
Miss Eleanor Glenn, Roma.
Mrs. Elizabeth Daniels, Chicago.

BIBLIOGRAFIA

(Alzetta, Manlio). L'Avvenire d'Italia, 12 Luglio, 1966.
Arlandi, Gian Franco. Presentazione, Catalogo, Galleria Numero, Milano, Roma, Venezia, 1966.
Art Digest, New York, May 15, 1945.
Art Institute of Chicago Quarterly, The. September 15, 1955.
Art News, New York, December 1, 1950.
Baldini, Umberto. La Nazione, Firenze, 28 Maggio, 1965.
Barry, Edward. Chicago Sunday Tribune, July 24, 1966.
Bertocco, Evangelina (Emmanuel). « Il Violino della Scultrice », Minose, Venezia 30 Luglio, 1966.

Blackshear Kathleen. The Bulletin of the Art Institute of Chicago, December, 1947.
Bovi, A. Il Messaggero, Roma, 30 Maggio, 1965.
Brittanica Junior, Chicago, 1961, Vol. 5, p. 172 (reprs.)
Bulliet, C.J. The Art Digest, New York, February 1, 1951.
Burg, Copeland C. Chicago Herald-American, November 4, 1952.
— November 10, 1952.
Butler, Doris Lane. Chicago Daily News, August 4, 1958.
— September 15, 1958.
— Chicago Daily News « Weekend », October 4, 1958 (repr.)
Buttafava, Riccardo. Arte Cristiana, Milano, Ottobre, 1966.
Camphell, Larry. Art News, New York, January, 1951.
Chicago Daily News, October 31, 1952.
— April 28, 1960 (repr.)
Chicago Herald-American, December 12, 1952.
Chicago Musical College Quarterly, March, 1953.
Chicago Sun Times, December 8, 1950 (repr.)
— October 4, 1953.
— June 9, 1957 (repr.).
— June 5, 1967 (repr.).
Chicago Tribune, February 2, 1951.
— November 12, 1951.
— June 4, 1953 (repr.).
— May 16, 1954.
— June 2, 1957 (repr.).
— March 13, 1958 (repr.).
— June 1, 1958 (repr.).
— June 26, 1958.
— June 21, 1959 (repr.).
— July 5, 1963.
— Jannuary 12, 1964.
— April 19, 1964.
— November 27, 1966.
— March 5, 1968 (repr.).
Christian Art, Chicago, July 1965 (repr.).
— November, 1966.
Coletti, Virgilio. Programma, Galleria Numero, Milano, Roma, Venezia 1966.
Corriere della Sera, Milano, 27 Aprile 1966.
Dame, Lawrence. « Regarding Art », Boston Sunday Herald, July 15, 1945.
— July 14, 1946.
— April 30, 1950.
— June 24, 1951.
Dauphiné, Le, Grenoble.
— 10 Mars, 1968 (repr.).
Devries, René. Musical Courier, New York, Jannuary 1, 1953.
Documenti di Numero, Firenze, No. 2, 1966 (reprs.).
— No. 3, 1966 (reprs.).
Driscoll, Jr. Edgar J. Boston Sunday Globe, May 1, 1949.
Durney, Helen. « Review, Gallery Book for Children: Twelve Paintings and Related Works of Art » by Marie Zoe Greene, Design, Indianapolis, Indiana, November, 1941.
Duxbury Clipper (Massachusetts), June, 1951.
— July 15, 1965 (repr.).
Eighth Annual Religious Art Show, Catalogue. Baptist Graduate Student Center, Chicago, 1967 (repr.).

Elgar, Frank. Carrefour, Paris, 19 Juin, 1963.
— 5 Mai, 1965.
— 29 Juin, 1966.
Espiau, Marcel. Nouveaux Jours, Paris, 7 Juin, 1963.
Evening Citizen, The, Ottawa, Canada, April 23, 1946.
Fabbri, Giuseppe. Corriere di Sicilia, Catania, 1 Ottobre, 1966.
Friedlander, Alberta, Chicago Daily News. March 26, 1960.
— June 25, 1960.
— December 24, 1960.
— April 22, 1961.
Gazzetino, 11 Venezia, 13 Giugno, 1966.
— 4 Luglio, 1966.
Gigli, Guglielmo. Minosse, Venezia, 2 Luglio 1966.
— Pensiero ed Arte, Bari, 12 Giugno 1966.
Greene-Mercier, Marie Zoe.
Marie Zoe E. Mercier. Ave Roma, The Commonweal, New York, September 4, 1929.
— The North Portal of Notre Dame de Chartres, Ave Maria, Notre Dame, Indiana August 30, 1930.
— Eastertide in Rome, The Commonweal, April 8, 1931.
— La Cupola, The Commonweal, March 30, 1932.
— The Mother, The Commonweal, July 7, 1933.
— The Monsignore, The Commonweal, March 30, 1934.
— The Museum of Modern Art, The Commonweal, February 15, 1935.
— Defense of Unintelligibility: review of « The Meaning of Unintelligibity in Modern Art » by Edward F. Rothschild, University of Chicago Press, The Commonweal, March 1, 1935.
— A Modern Painter: review of « Seurat and the Evolution of the Grande Jatte » by Daniel Catton Rich, University of Chicago Press, The Commonweal, May 8, 1936.
Marie Zoe Greene. For Children: the Exhibition of Masterpieces of Italian Art lent by the Italian Government, Department of Education, the Art Institute of Chicago, 1939.
— Gallery Book for Children: Twelve Paintings and Related Works of Art in the Collections of the Art Institute of Chicago, Department of Education, the Art Institute of Chicago, 1940.
— The Primacy of Evocation, Liturgical Arts Quarterly, New York, February, 1958. (reprs.)
Marie Zoe Greene-Mercier, Second International Exposition of Sacred Art Trieste, Italy, Christian Art, Chicago, November, 1967 (reprs.).
Haydon, Harold. Chicago Sun Times, April 9, 1967.
— June 11, 1967.
— June 18, 1967.
— September 10, 1967.
Holland, Frank. Chicago Sun Times, October 17, 1946.
— November 11, 1951.
— October 4, 1953.
— April 18, 1954.
— June 27, 1954.
— July 3, 1955
— February 12, 1956.
— April 1, 1956.
— March 10, 1957.
— April 1, 1958.
— April 13, 1958.
— September 21, 1958 (repr.).
— March 20, 1960.

— April 30, 1961 (repr.).

— April 15, 1962.

— May 10, 1963.

Hyde Park Herald, Chicago, October 20, 1949.

— August 23, 1967 (repr.).

Information, L', Paris 7 Juin, 1963 (repr.).

Israel-Mayer, Daniel. Arts, Paris, 12 Juin, 1963.

Jewett, Eleanor. Chicago Sunday Tribune, February 18, 1951.

— February 4, 1951.

— February 5, 1956.

— February 12, 1956.

Journal de l'Amateur d'Art, Paris, 25 Juin, 1963.

Lanzuolo, Anna. Vogue e Novità, Milano, Maggio, 1956 (repr.).

Lavanoux, Maurice. Editor's Diary, Liturgical Arts Quarterly, New York, February, 1967. (repr.).

Lawton, Alice. Boston Sunday Post, June 30, 1946.

Levy, Pesella. Art Digest, December 1, 1950.

Lipchitz, Jacques. Marie Zoe Greene-Mercier, Quaderni della Galleria S. Stefano, Venezia, 1968.

Meridional de Marseille, Le, (J.C.R.), 10 Mars, 1968 (repr.).

Metcalf, Margaret C. Quintessential, privately printed, Boston, Massachusetts, 1954 (repr.).

Milan, B. Apollo, Bruxelles, Décembre, 1963. (repr.).

Miller, Lucy Key. Chicago Daily Tribune, April 4, 1955.

Milwaukee Journal (Wisconsin), March 18, 1951.

— March 27, 1951 (repr).

Milwaukee Sentinel (Wisconsin), March 14, 1951.

— March 29, 1951 (repr.).

Minosse, Venezia, 9 Luglio, 1966.

— 16 Luglio, 1966.

Moholy-Nagy, L. The New Vision, revised and enlarged, 1938, W. W. Norton, New York, (repr.) Fig. 105a.

— The New Vision, 4th revised edition, 1947, George Wittenborn, Inc. New York, (repr.) p. 44.

Montreal Daily Star, March 29, 1945.

Montreal Gazette, No, 264, 1945.

Musical Courier, New York, January 15, 1957, p. 115 (repr.).

New York Daily News, Marchs, 1968 (repr.).

New York Herald Tribune, December 3, 1950.

New York Times, December 3, 1954.

O' Connor, Jean. Chicago Daily News, August 24, 1966 (repr.).

Orlando, Bruno. La Vita Nuova, Trieste, 30 Settembre, 1966.

— Documentazione della Seconda Mostra Internazionale d'Arte Sacra, Trieste, 1967 (repr.).

Ovresat, Raymond C. Chicago Chapter Bulletin, American Institute of Architects, July, 1957 (reprs.).

Parnell, Dorothy. Milwaukee Sentinel (Wisconsin), March 12, 1954.

Pascal, R.C. Le Dauphiné, 10 Mars, 1968.

Philpott, A.J. This Week in the Art World, Boston Sunday Globe, May 4, 1947.

Piccolo, II, Trieste, 21 Settembre, 1966.

Preston, Stuart. The New York Times, Dicember 3, 1950.

Radcliffe Quarterly, Cambridge, Massachusetts, May 1946 (repr.).

Redcliffe Re-News, Cambridge, October, 1952. (repr.).

Revue Moderne, La, Paris, 1 Juillet, 1963.

Riccobaldi, G. Il Nuovo Cittadino, Genova, 22 Ottobre, 1966.

Rood, John. Sculpture With a Torch, University of Minnesota Press, (Minneapolis) 1963, p. 91 (repr.).

Saint-Evremond, France-Amérique, New York, 16 Juin, 1963 (repr.).

Salon de la Jeune Sculpture, Catalogue, Paris, 1965 (repr.).

Salon Internationale de la Femme, III ème, Cannes, 1968 (repr.).

Settimana a Roma, La, (Pan), 12 Giugno, 1966 (repr.).

Southeast Economist, Chicago, January 9, 1964.

Southwest Standard, Southwest Missouri State College (Springfield), September 29, 1950.

Springfield Leader and Press (Missouri), September 18, 1950.

Sweet, Frederick A. Foreword, Exhibition Catalogue, Westwinds Bookshop and Gallery, Duxbury, Massachusetts, 1951.

Tourette, Jean. La Marseillaise, Marseilles, 22 Mars, 1968.

Tourtelot, Madeline. Chicago American, February 5, 1958.

Treat, Priscilla Gough. To Be Noted, Radcliffe Quarterly, Cambridge, Massachusetts, August, 1964.

— May 1965.

— February, 1967.

Trier, Marilyn Robb. Art News, New York, January 1953 (repr.).

— May, 1955.

Uretz, Vi Fogle. Chicago Artist, Marie Zoe Greene, WFMT Fine Arts Guide, Chicago February, 1956 (reprs.).

Vieillefond, Jean René. Presentazione, Catalogo, Galleria d'Arte Arno, Firenze, 1965.

Warnod, Jeanne. Le Figaro, Paris, 6 Juin, 1963.

Weigle, Edith, Chicago Sunday Tribune, July 13, 1958 (repr.).

— March 27, 1960.

— April, 1961.

— June 20, 1965 (repr.).

Weitzel, Tony. Chicago Daily News, June 22, 1960.

Weller, Allen S. The Art Digest, New York, December 1, 1952.

FOTOGRAPHERS

Barker, Barsotti, Boccardi, Del Bocca, Fortunati, Press Color, Porter, Publi Foto, Kakehashi, Sbarge.

Finito di stampare nel mese di giugno 1968
nello Stabilimento delle Arti Grafiche D'Urso
Vicolo Sciarra, 62 - Roma